COMMON
WISDOM
Journal

COMMON
WISDOM
Journal

Dive deeper into your personal
journey with this journal

LAURA GABAYAN, MD, MS

Published by:
Redwood Publishing, LLC
www.redwooddigitalpublishing.com
Orange County, California

ISBN: 978-1-966333-03-6 (paperback)

Interior Design: Jose Pepito
Cover Design: Michelle Manley, Graphique Designs

CONTENTS

WELCOME!

WELCOME TO A JOURNAL THAT WILL HELP START YOUR journey of living your best life. The reason I wrote this journal is because I have found that, while my book and work focus on defining wisdom, understanding wisdom is not relevant to many. What I found is that the eight elements are really the secret ingredients to living a great life.

I am a physician and a researcher who, until 2013, had published extensively in academia. My world was centered around science and medicine. I was most comfortable in that world. Diagnosing, fixing, quantifying, and explaining medical and scientific results helped me make sense of my world. Then, my body began to deteriorate. Physically moving in the simplest of ways became impossible. My body was failing me. And so was science. The two things I counted on and took for granted were letting me down. My diagnosis and treatments became a nightmare. There wasn't much I could do about my physical issues, but I could change *how I thought about* all of this. I needed to shift my paradigm. It was time to look outside of my comfort zone. I needed a new perspective.

I decided to combine my scientific expertise with my quest for new perspectives. I wanted to better understand the people who look at life through a wider lens and who are open to new ideas and perspectives—the wise. Before I approached these wise individuals, I needed to research what wisdom is, how different cultures defined it, or if it was even definable. What I found was the information we already had about wisdom was either anecdotal or subjective. As a scientist, I needed more objectivity, so I created a scientific study, The Wisdom Research Project, and wrote a book based on my findings titled *Common Wisdom*. For the project, I interviewed sixty adults from all across North America, aged fifty to seventy-nine, who were considered wise by the people who knew them. Then, a team of us evaluated my interviews and arrived at the traits the interviewees had in common. As a result, I was able to scientifically define wisdom as eight interconnected elements. These elements are Resilience, Kindness, Positivity, Spirituality, Humility, Tolerance, Creativity, and Curiosity (ranked in that order). Only one interviewee had all eight elements; the others had various combinations of each.

From our results, what became very clear was that incorporating these eight elements into our lives leads to more joy, peace, happiness, and success. They allow us to be the best version of ourselves. By diving deep into each element and really thinking honestly about how each one fits into our lives, we can identify which are our strengths and which may need a little bit of work. Helping sort through all of this is the purpose of this journal. Working in conjunction with the book *Common Wisdom*, this journal is your opportunity to learn more about yourself, discover your strengths and weaknesses regarding these elements, and determine new ways to incorporate them into your daily lives in very practical ways. This journal will help you to actively improve your life, bring more meaning and fulfillment into it, and help to create stronger relationships.

HOW TO USE
THIS JOURNAL

THIS JOURNAL IS MEANT TO HAVE YOU REFLECT ON THE eight elements in an enjoyable and mindful way, helping you to become a better version of yourself. You may not immediately "see" or "feel" a difference, but know that it is happening.

As with any new endeavor, the more you practice, the better the results. You can spend as little or as much time as you want reflecting on each element. You can journal in it every day or once a week, whatever fits your lifestyle. Every so often, you may want to look back at your responses to the questions to see just how far you've come.

Each section describes the element and has some insights from the book *Common Wisdom*. It also has a few quotes mentioned in the book. It includes some of the "Things to Ask Yourself" questions from the book as well as additional prompts to get you thinking more deeply about the element.

Welcome to the start of a new life! Know that the process of you understanding and applying these elements will take time, so be patient and kind to yourself. You have taken the first step by investing in this journal, so be proud of yourself.

RESILIENCE

THE MOST IMPORTANT ELEMENT OF WISDOM WAS IDEN-
tified as Resilience, which is the idea that, regardless of
the obstacle, we keep moving forward; we do not give up.
We are warriors, not victims. As Dolly Parton said, "If you
want the rainbow, you gotta put up with the rain." With
every obstacle comes lessons, leading to greater wisdom.
Instead of thinking, "Why me?" think, "Why not me?"

Obstacles are emotionally difficult, but they are abso-
lutely surmountable. Differentiating the emotions from
the difficulty is a great first step. Instead of focusing
on the problem, focusing on the solution is an active
way of staying out of negative emotions. Also, when
encountering an obstacle, interviewees talked about the
importance of being "fiercely flexible." Remind yourself
that things don't happen *to* you but *for* you. Obstacles
help build our mental muscle and prove that a difficulty
can be overcome.

1. What does resilience mean to you?

_____

_____

_____

_____

_____

2. How important is resilience to you and your life?

_____

_____

_____

_____

_____

3. Why is acceptance an important part of resilience?

_____

_____

_____

_____

_____

4. How are fear and resilience related?

_____

_____

_____

_____

5. Have you heard the term "spiritual surrender"? What does it mean, and how is it related to resilience?

_____

_____

_____

_____

_____

6. How are resilience and success in life related?

_____

_____

_____

_____

_____

7. What does it mean to *not* be resilient to you?

_____

_____

_____

_____

8. How can your reaction impact others around you in emotionally charged situations?

_____

_____

_____

_____

9. How quickly are you able to adapt to a challenging situation?

_____

_____

_____

_____

10. What does being flexible mean to you?

_____

_____

_____

_____

11. How flexible would those closest to you say you are?

_____

_____

_____

_____

12. How often have you been emotionally "thrown" by unexpected news in the last year? How did you handle it? Looking back, how could you have handled it better?

_____

_____

_____

_____

13. How do your own positive or negative emotions affect your everyday life?

_____

_____

_____

_____

14. How do you view an obstacle?

_____

_____

_____

15. How do you react to a last-minute change in plans or appointments?

_____

_____

_____

_____

16. What is one thing you can do to improve your resilience?

_____

_____

_____

_____

17. What support do you have that can help you overcome obstacles? It can be a person or a thing.

_____

_____

_____

_____

18. Have things changed in the past months or years so that your thoughts are different about the above?

_____

_____

_____

_____

KINDNESS

Kindness was the next most important element, according to our interviewees. It was not only how they interacted with the world, but it was how they treated themselves. They also mentioned that it was important to surround yourself with kindness. Being kind has far-reaching implications and shows that you respect others. We all deserve respect.

Kindness is something those around you will always remember, and as Mark Twain once said, "Kindness is the language which the deaf can hear and the blind can see." When given from the heart, kindness makes a big impact with very little effort.

1. How important is kindness to you? Why?

_____

_____

_____

_____

_____

2. What does being kind mean to you?

_____

_____

_____

_____

_____

3. How do you perceive a person who is kind? Why?

_____

_____

_____

_____

_____

4. How can kindness impact one's effectiveness in communication?

_____

_____

_____

_____

5. What are the impacts of a kind act?

_____

_____

_____

_____

6. How can kindness affect a negotiation?

_____

_____

_____

_____

7. Are there situations in which being kind is especially difficult? Explain.

_____

_____

_____

_____

8. Is self-care a form of kindness? Why or why not?

_____

_____

_____

_____

9. Why do you "catch more flies with honey than with vinegar"?

_____

_____

_____

_____

10. What is the kindest thing someone has ever done for you?

_____

_____

_____

_____

11. What is the kindest thing you have done for someone else anonymously?

_____

_____

_____

_____

12. What simple acts of kindness can you adopt in your life starting today?

_____

_____

_____

_____

13. Can you remember an incident where you failed to show kindness and now regret it?

_____

_____

_____

_____

14. What is one thing you can do to show yourself kindness?

_____

_____

_____

_____

15. What does forgiveness mean to you?

_____

_____

_____

_____

16. What do you think about the term "forgive and forget"?

_____

_____

_____

_____

_____

17. Have things changed in the past months or years so that your thoughts are different about the above?

_____

_____

_____

_____

_____

POSITIVITY

POSITIVITY WAS THE THIRD MOST PREVALENT ELEMENT. It is about perspective. While we can't control our environment, we can control our thoughts. Positivity attracts positivity and can often counter negativity. We deserve to be happy. It not only feels good to be positive, but it can also improve your health and well-being.

Two large subthemes of positivity were gratitude and humor. For years, gratitude has been found to be a large part of wisdom because it helps people overcome obstacles with more ease by serving as a type of forced appreciation. The reason journals such as this exist is to help people discover and clarify the many positive aspects of their lives that may have been lost or forgotten. Humor also helps people lower their stress, depression, and anxiety. It can even help improve self-esteem. Not to mention help overcome difficulties by adding more levity to the situation.

1. What role does positivity play in your life?

_____

_____

_____

_____

2. Are you a "glass half full" or "glass half empty" kind of person? Why do you think that is?

_____

_____

_____

_____

_____

3. How do you feel when being around positive people? What about negative people?

_____

_____

_____

_____

4. How does your physical body and posture impact your state of positivity?

_____

_____

_____

_____

5. How can loving and respecting yourself impact your positivity?

_____

_____

_____

_____

6. How have social media and the internet impacted your positivity?

_____

_____

_____

_____

7. Why is gratitude so important in life?

_____

_____

_____

_____

_____

8. How does gratitude help one overcome negativity?

_____

_____

_____

_____

9. How can you practice gratitude every day? If you already practice gratitude, how can you increase your gratitude?

_____

_____

_____

10. Are you someone who takes yourself seriously? If so, what if you were to be more lighthearted? How would you feel?

_____

_____

_____

11. Does "not sweating the small stuff" impact your perspective?

_____

_____

_____

_____

_____

12. How can focusing on productivity impact one's positivity?

_____

_____

_____

_____

13. When faced with a challenge, how do you use positivity to overcome that challenge?

_____

_____

_____

_____

_____

14. How can expectations stifle positivity?

_____

_____

_____

15. How are expectations different than goals?

_____

_____

_____

_____

16. How can you use more humor in your life?

_____

_____

_____

_____

_____

_____

17. What do you feel about being funny? Whether it's you or someone else.

_____

_____

_____

_____

_____

_____

_____

18. How do you think others will perceive you if you are funny? Will it change the way you view yourself?

_____

_____

_____

_____

_____

19. Have things changed in the past months or years so that your thoughts are different about the above?

_____

_____

_____

_____

_____

SPIRITUALITY

SPIRITUALITY, THE BELIEF THAT A HIGHER POWER EX-ists, was the fourth element. This higher power is not something that can be seen in our physical world, but that does not mean it does not exist. This higher power can be called various terms, such as the universe, the divine, the Great Spirit, or God. It can be viewed differently by all of us. As John Lennon said, "I believe in God, but not as one thing, not as an old man in the sky. I believe that what people call God is something in all of us."

Spirituality has been an important component of people's lives for thousands of years. It is different than religiosity. Spirituality is the feeling that some unseen power is watching over us or guiding us through our lives. This belief brings us comfort and peace. It also allows for deeper connections with others.

1. How are spirituality and religiosity different? Can you be one and not the other?

_____

_____

_____

_____

2. Do you have to see something to believe it exists?

_____

_____

_____

_____

3. Can one have mixed feelings toward this higher power but still believe that it exists?

_____

_____

_____

_____

4. How does spirituality bring meaning and depth to life?

_____

_____

_____

_____

5. Is there something you do that gives you an unusual feeling or satisfaction that can only be explained spiritually, such as volunteering or serving as a mentor?

_____

_____

_____

_____

6. How does curiosity influence spirituality?

_____

_____

_____

_____

7. Has something happened in your life or the life of another person that has made you more spiritual?

_____

_____

_____

_____

8. How do you explain the instant connection you have with someone or your gut feeling about something or someone?

_____

_____

_____

9. Have you seen "miracles" that seem to be impossible? How did those happen?

_____

_____

_____

_____

10. Is this higher power benevolent or malevolent?

_____

_____

_____

_____

11. Can being spiritual give you a greater sense of inner peace? How?

_____

_____

_____

_____

_____

12. How do you explain tragedy happening to a good person?

_____

_____

_____

_____

13. Is prayer part of your life? If not, how can you make it part of your life?

_____

_____

_____

_____

_____

_____

14. It's said that prayer greatly benefits the one praying. How so?

_____

_____

_____

_____

_____

_____

15. How can having faith that "things will work out" give you more comfort and inner peace?

_____

_____

_____

_____

16. Can something that seems "negative" really be positive?

_____

_____

_____

_____

17. Have things changed in the past months or years so that your thoughts are different about the above?

_____

_____

_____

_____

HUMILITY

HUMILITY WAS THE FIFTH ELEMENT AND IS A VIRTUE that has been recognized throughout time. Yet now, with the age of social media, it has taken a backseat to an almost pathological need to show off. Humility allows for better social connections and a heightened sense of emotional intelligence. It is not the absence of self-esteem but rather not putting yourself on a pedestal above others.

A humble person is down-to-earth. They are confident and secure while being open to other ideas and constructive criticism. Making others feel small does not make them feel big. As C.S. Lewis believed, they do not think less of themselves but think of themselves less.

1. Does humility have a role in your life? Have you thought about its value?

_____

_____

_____

_____

2. How can being humble impact your life?

_____

_____

_____

3. How open are you to learning from others? Do you always have to be right?

_____

_____

_____

_____

4. When someone feels confident and secure, why is it easier for them to be humble?

_____

_____

_____

_____

5. How does being humble help you connect with others?

_____

_____

_____

_____

6. What is one example of when you felt your needs were more important than someone else's?

_____

_____

_____

_____

7. How can being humble allow for personal growth?

_____

_____

_____

_____

8. Do you enjoy being around someone who is humble? If so, why?

_____

_____

_____

_____

9. How is being humble related to being kind?

_____

_____

_____

_____

10. How is being humble related to having emotional intelligence?

_____

_____

_____

_____

11. What does success mean to you?

_____

_____

_____

_____

12. How accurate are you in recognizing your own short-comings and limitations?

_____

_____

_____

_____

13. How are humility and spirituality related?

_____

_____

_____

_____

_____

_____

1.4 We have seen a shift away from humility in today's world. Why do you think that is?

_____

_____

_____

_____

_____

_____

_____

15. How can having an ego or pride be destructive to oneself and others?

_____

_____

_____

_____

_____

_____

16. Have things changed in the past months or years so that your thoughts are different about the above?

_____

_____

_____

_____

_____

_____

TOLERANCE

Tolerance, the sixth element, is the ability to keep an open mind and be considerate of different cultures, ideas, and experiences. A tolerant person is open-minded and considerate of other perspectives. Being tolerant also allows for better social connections.

By being tolerant, we respect other opinions and are not judgmental or prejudiced. A tolerant person realizes that we are all important and deserve respect. It's never too late to become more tolerant and, as Henry David Thoreau said, "give up your prejudices." Two subthemes of tolerance were patience and flexibility.

1. How effectively do you handle a situation where you strongly disagree with someone else's opinion?

_____

_____

_____

_____

2. Have you ever been able to change a strongly held opinion of yours because you listened and/or learned from someone else's differing opinion?

_____

_____

_____

_____

3. How does being tolerant of other ideas affect your own ideas? Does it mean you forego your own?

_____

_____

_____

_____

4. How does being tolerant increase self-esteem?

_____

_____

_____

_____

_____

5. How does being tolerant allow us to be more spiritual?

_____

_____

_____

_____

6. Have you ever been a "target" of intolerance? How did you handle it?

_____

_____

_____

_____

7. What is one thing you know you are intolerant of? Why do you think that is?

_____

_____

_____

_____

_____

8. Despite the age of the internet and more information sharing, we seem more intolerant and polarized than ever. Why is that?

_____

_____

_____

_____

9. How is having patience a form of tolerance?

_____

_____

_____

10. How do you deal with delays? Such as delays in deliveries or delays in deadlines?

_____

_____

_____

_____

11. When encountering a challenge, how can being flexible change your perspective of the challenge?

_____

_____

_____

_____

12. Have things changed in the past months or years so that your thoughts are different about the above?

_____

_____

_____

_____

CREATIVITY

CREATIVITY, THE SEVENTH ELEMENT, IS AN INNATE property that we all have had since childhood. It allows for imagination that goes beyond possibilities. It is essential to our growth as a people and gets us out of survival mode. Being creative allows us to question what *is* and then think about what *could be*.

We are all different from one another and thus express our creativity in different ways. This can range from the way we talk and dress to the way we live. Being creative in their roles in life was a large subtheme of the interviewees. They wore many hats and had many roles in life.

1. How creative are you in your life? Is it important to you to be creative?

_____

_____

_____

_____

2. What is the most creative thing you have done or thought about in the last week?

_____

_____

_____

_____

3. How do other people you know express their creativity that you appreciate?

_____

_____

_____

_____

4. How do you use creativity at work and/or at home?

_____

_____

_____

_____

_____

5. What hats do you wear that makes you creative in life? Can you wear more hats?

_____

_____

_____

_____

_____

6. What is one childlike thing you miss doing as an adult?

_____

_____

_____

_____

7. How does creativity get us out of survival mode? Similarly, how can being in survival mode affect creativity?

_____

_____

_____

8. If money or responsibilities were not an issue, is there a creative act you would love to do in your life?

_____

_____

_____

_____

9. Doing "nothing" can spark your creativity. Why can that time actually lead to productive thoughts?

_____

_____

_____

_____

10. Despite our modern luxuries, doing "nothing" is increasingly difficult. Is there something you can change in your life so that you have more of that "empty" time?

_____

_____

_____

11. Is there something that pushes you to be more creative? Can you do more of that "something"?

_____

_____

_____

_____

12. Have things changed in the past months or years so that your thoughts are different about the above?

_____

_____

_____

_____

CURIOSITY

Curiosity was the eighth and final element in my study. Although it was the final element, it serves as the driving force of all the other elements. It allows for change, growth, and discovery. Similar to creativity, having curiosity is an innate talent we have all possessed since childhood.

Being curious means never taking things at face value and questioning the most obvious and simple concepts. This thirst for differing perspectives is something Mark Twain emphasized when he said, "Whenever you find yourself on the side of the majority, it is time to pause and reflect."

1. How can you incorporate more curiosity into your life? At work or at home?

_____

_____

_____

_____

2. Are you interested in how others think or how things are made or work? Why or why not?

_____

_____

_____

_____

3. When someone tells you a "fact" or a story, do you question the source?

_____

_____

_____

_____

4. When you encounter something new, would you rather do the same thing you always do or explore?

_____

_____

_____

_____

5. How does being curious help one have better social connections?

_____

_____

_____

_____

6. Many adults do not feel they have the time or patience to explore. Is that what you feel? If so, can exploration and inquiry become more of a part of your life?

_____

_____

_____

7. Do you tend to accept things at face value, or do you find yourself questioning everything you are told?

_____

_____

_____

_____

8. What is something you've always wondered about but never bothered to pursue?

_____

_____

_____

_____

9. How can wondering about the metaphysical help you become more spiritual?

_____

_____

_____

_____

10. Being curious is often stunted by fear. Do you find that your fear stops you from being curious?

_____

_____

_____

_____

11. Being curious can help you be more hopeful. How?

_____

_____

_____

_____

12. Have things changed in the past months or years so that your thoughts are different about the above?

_____

_____

_____

_____

KEEP MOVING FORWARD

Congratulations on completing your journal. This is the first step in improving yourself and your life. Now that you have taken stock of each of the various elements of wisdom, it is time to incorporate this new insight into your daily life in a practical and meaningful way. Taking a few minutes each day to reflect on where you are and where you would like to be regarding these elements will keep you moving forward toward your goal of living a life with greater meaning and fulfillment.

Taking time to reflect on where you have been is a powerful way to see just how far you have come. The road each of us travels throughout our lives is long, and it is easy to lose track of where we began this journey and where we are going. So, every so often, take a look at what you have written on these pages and see if you are continuing to move forward. Look to see if you would answer any of these questions differently, knowing what you know now, and how your new life experiences have impacted you since first answering these questions.

Thinking about and recognizing the importance of these elements is the beginning of your path to a better life.

Keep moving forward.